DEDICATION

For David, whose appreciation of the great outdoors and love of northern Michigan inspired this book.

And, for Bryce, Brady, Melanie, Mike and Eleanor – my family – the heart and soul of my life.

CHARI YOST BINSTADT

For all of us... young at heart. "It's okay to play."

KEN SCOTT

Up North in Michigan

Chari Yost Binstadt TEXT

Ken Scott PHOTOGRAPHY

Petunia Press PUBLISHER

I love being up north in Michigan.

always **smile** just **thinking about it.**

Each season has
things to see and
things to do
that are special.

For me one of the best signs that **summer has arrived,** is getting the dock

out in the lake.

It's like an invitation to

jump
in the water!

ready! set! go!

The **sand dunes** are a favorite place of mine. Sometimes I climb to the top and then collapse in the sand to catch my breath. Then we like to **race all the way down!!**

We like to go to the shore of the **big lake** and walk along the beach looking for petoskey stones. Michigan is the **only place in the world** where they can be found. I learned that the pattern on them is really tiny fossils that are **millions of years old!**

I like to keep
a small petoskey stone
in my pocket
for good luck.

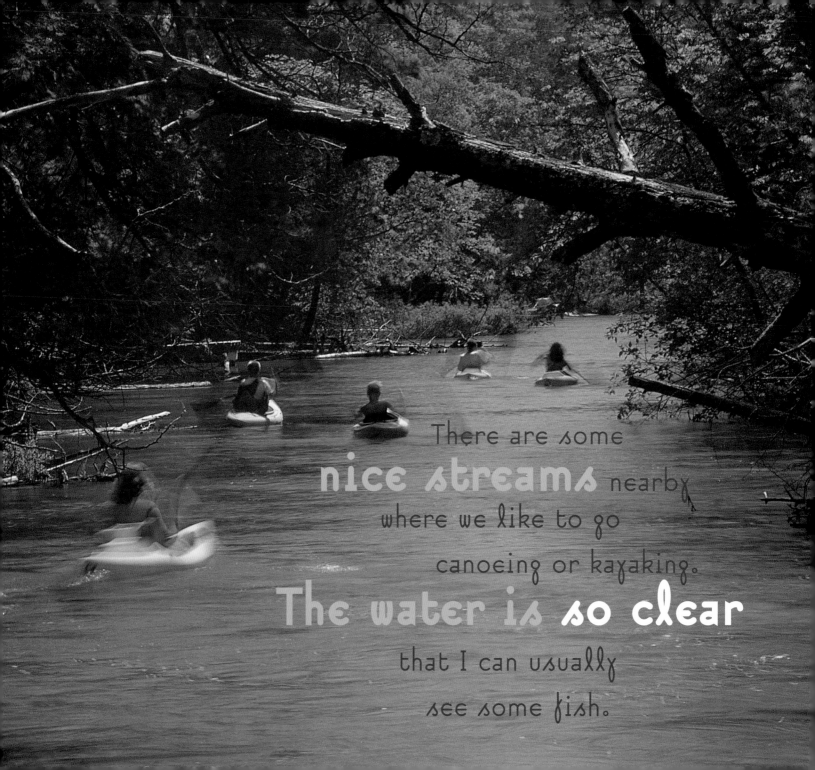

There are some **nice streams** nearby where we like to go canoeing or kayaking. **The water is so clear** that I can usually see some fish.

There are sailboats of all sizes on the lakes and in the harbors. The bright sails look so pretty out on the blue water.

Mom promised that she and I could learn to sail together.

We usually go to a parade on the

Fourth of July.

One year, I decorated my bike
and rode it in the parade.

It was so much fun!

We always stay up to watch the **fireworks**.

I go swimming
almost every day
in the summer.

Sometimes when we go to the beach,
we take our lunch in a picnic basket.

I could stay all day
playing in the sand
and cooling off in
the water.

The sand castles
we build get
bigger each year.

There are *so many fun things to do.* I never run out of ideas. Sometimes, though, I like to do nothing but lie back and watch the Michigan clouds in the sky.

Almost every day,
we stop at the
roadside stands
for summer treats.

We always get a lot of

I like to get
fresh blueberries
to put in our pancakes
at breakfast.

Later in the summer,
we can get sweet corn that
melts in our mouths.
It is so good!

Michigan cherries.

Last summer,
Grandpa and I
drove to a small, quiet lake to go fishing. That was the first time **I saw a loon,** and heard its unusual call.

We sat quietly and watched the loon in the distance as the sun was setting. I'm glad there are quiet lakes in Michigan so that loons will always live here.

I always **keep my eyes open** and watch carefully when Grandma and I walk down the lane to the mailbox. We see so many different kinds of **birds.** I think they like the birdfeeders we have nearby! Once, we saw a

raccoon perched up in a tree. Another time, we saw a **baby fox** near the side of the road. Sometimes, we will surprise a **deer** and watch as it runs off into the woods. I love picking up the mail with **Grandma!**

After dinner, my family and I
almost always watch the sunset.
Sometimes we sit on
top of a sand dune.
Sometimes we like to be at the beach.
It doesn't really matter where we are.

The sunsets
are
awesome.

On special nights, after dark,

have a **campfire near the water.**

We might tell stories or sing songs and roast marshmallows. On very clear nights, I like to lie back and see how many shooting stars I can count. One time, the sky was all lit up and it looked as if the lights were dancing.

It was amazing. It was the Northern Lights.

There are
so many trees
up north. Can you imagine what
it is like in the fall when
all of the leaves start turning
yellow, red and **orange?**

When we take a
walk or ride our bikes
along some of the
roads, I feel like I am in a **bright, colorful**

tunnel.

The trees in the apple orchards
are filled with fruit in the fall.
Michigan has a lot of

different kinds
of apples.

When we go to
the fruit stand, we get some to
eat and some for making the

best apple pie

anyone has ever tasted.

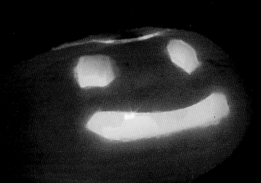

In October,
we see fields of bright orange pumpkins.
There are all different sizes and shapes.
It's fun to choose the ones we want to carve for

Halloween.

Did you know that there are black squirrels up north?

When the leaves
are falling from
the trees,
and the animals are
busy getting ready for winter,
I start getting excited
for the
first snowfall.
When it comes,
I bundle up and
race outside
to build a
snowman.

Holiday time is filled with
sights, sounds, and smells
that I love. The pretty lights,
the snow crunching under our boots,
the jingle bells and the music,
the freshly cut evergreen,
the smell of cookies baking...
it's a great time to
be up north.

When there is **enough snow** on the ground, I put on my cross-country skis or my snowshoes and **go exploring.**

We love to go to one of the nearby hills and **go sledding.** I put on my warmest clothes so I can stay a long time!

I love to look for **frogs** in the spring.
The best sound is
frogs chirping in the evenings
by the ponds.
We call those frogs **peepers**,
because of the sounds they make.

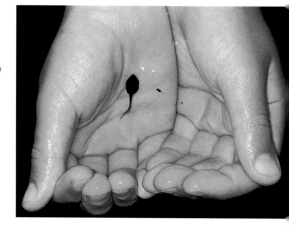

Every year, at the same pond,
we see a mother and father swan
with at least one baby swan.
Dad told me that
baby swans are called
cygnets.

For a few weeks in May, the woods are filled with **pretty, white wildflowers** called trillium. There are so many you can't even count them all.

If I look carefully, I might see
a wildflower called a
showy lady's-slipper. I don't ever
pick them. If we leave them
alone, then maybe next year
there will be more of them.

In the spring, when the sky is blue,
and the sun is shining, and
the cherry trees are in bloom,
and I go to the top of a hill
and look way out across the blue lake,
I know I am in one of the

prettiest places
in the whole world.

When the birds are making
their nests, and the butterflies are
flying from tree to tree,
I know that summer is not far away.

Maybe one day we'll get inner tubes
and float down one of the rivers.

Maybe we'll take a ferry
to Mackinac Island.